To Huw

The New Blur Album

John Osborne

Enjoy!

Nasty Little Press

Published by Nasty Little Press in July 2011.

35 St Johns Road, Bungay, Suffolk

nastylittlepress.org

Printed and bound by Print-X
7 Edgefield Close, Whitchurch, Bristol

ISBN: 978-0-9563767-7-0

A CIP record of this book is available
from the British Library.

Nasty Little Press is the proud recipient of a Grants for the Arts
Award from Arts Council England.

LOTTERY FUNDED

Acknowledgements

With thanks to Luke Wright, Sally Roe and Henry Layte at The Book Hive.

Contents

Surprise

It's you I feel sorry for.
You hired the room
and when no-one RSVP'd
you assumed my friends were too cool to RSVP
and ordered a finger buffet for fifty.

My surprise birthday party:
four of us,
me and you, your mum and dad.
When I told you once I don't like the idea of surprise parties
this was the kind of thing I had in mind.

"Maybe I put the wrong date on the invitations," you said,
as the waiter offered us yet more crabsticks.
We both knew you'd have triple-checked.
"Not even Graham," you said.
"Graham plays squash on Wednesdays," I said
and blew out the candles on the cake.

Under the table were bottles of wine,
thirty red and thirty white.
There wasn't even the chance to get a refund;
the receipt was in your handbag
that had been snatched that morning.

By the time we sang the happy birthday song
the waiter was so pissed he'll probably be fired
but anyone who can dance like that
is wasted in catering.

"What's it like not to have any friends?" your dad asked
and we all laughed apart from your mum
who still had her coat on.
"Maybe there's something good on the telly," he said.
I've never liked your dad
but last night he played a blinder
juggling satsumas as we looked out the of window.

It wasn't a special birthday.
I was 29, a prime number.
No-one gets excited about prime numbers,
but it reminded me of the time I was at Graham's house
when I pulled down my trousers and pants
and showed everyone the massive bruise on my knob.
I just thought more people would be interested.

Our waitress is Employee of the Month

Her photograph is in the foyer
and I imagine her pretending not to be bothered
when it was announced at the team meeting
a semi-circle of applause.

But the next morning she'd have shown her mum
the Twenty Pound High Street Voucher
and her mum would have said "Well done," and meant it,
because she knows it's important
to appreciate the small things.

And in town our waitress will have gone from shop to shop
content she didn't have to start work until half seven that evening.
Trying on a maxi dress in River Island
she'd wonder whether it was for the time
she helped an amputee cut up his food

managing to strike the perfect balance between being too fussy
and pretending she hadn't noticed.
She didn't even need to say anything like
"Shall I help you with that?"

it was just this intuition
she didn't even realise she had
and as she helped chop up his gammon and potatoes
he told her he was in town to see his daughter

who had just proposed to her boyfriend
taking advantage of the leap year
and he was so nervous he wouldn't get on
with his future son-in-law.
Our waitress would have asked if he'd like a dessert,

And at first he'd have said no
but she'd have said "Oh, go on!"
because she knows it's important to appreciate the small things.
She'd have smiled as he scooped up the last of his custard.

Our table is ready. The four of us take our seats
and as she hands out the menus
puts serviettes on our knees, she must know that we know,
we'd been in the foyer for so long, staring at her photograph

and I think: Please, no-one say anything,
don't let it be like the time we saw Dame Judi Dench
get out of a taxi by the Old Vic and shouted "Judi, Judi!"
until she turned and waved so awkwardly.

Let's just be grateful we're being served by
the Employee of the Month
and as she carries our plates of seabass
we know that if any of us start to choke on a bone
we will feel her arm around us.

Most people aren't that happy, anyway.

He buttons up his coat, walks to his car,
that transitory period between being a man at work
to putting coins into the hospital parking meter.

The first time he mentioned his son
on a kidney dialysis machine,
I thought: well, that explains why sometimes
I look up from my desk
and see him playing solitaire on his computer
letting the phone ring and ring.

Sometimes he'll come into the office and say "What's up, slags?"'
He'll say "What are you doing here Colin, you muppet?"
or "Why don't you return my calls, you pillock?"
but you can't judge people by what they do and say,
it's the way they sigh when they sit down on their chair.

Most people aren't that happy,
they're arguing about Iraq on internet forums
or phoning work at 9.05. "I've overslept again.
I'll be there as soon as I can."
They're asking if their spectacles
have been handed in at lost property,
they're at How To Quit Smoking seminars in church halls
or on the settee, waiting for their favourite programme to start,
not realising the series ended last week.

Of course there are people who have made it
Assistant Producers at Radio 1. Waitresses at The Ivy.
Holly Branson,
but most people aren't that happy
and no-one is going to say "Oh look, a portal,"
and you can close your eyes and jump
into a time before you lost your glasses,
when it was all four of you at home,
when this time you remembered to put the oven on

before you went for that walk
on Christmas afternoon.

Pages from Ceefax

"I'm worried about the future," I say,
racing a car around a Scalextric track.
Twitter trends with "Man worries about the future."
"What a loser!" some kid replies,
I spend the rest of the evening
correcting the typos on his website.

"There are too many television channels," I think,
watching a channel devoted to people discussing
whether there are too many television channels.
"I just liked it better in the old days," I tell the studio audience
when I am invited on the show.
A small section at the back applaud.

These are my people, I think, waving.
People who can't get to sleep at night
so read pages from Ceefax
as hot chocolate warms on the hob.

"There are too many blogs," I write on my blog
and immediately it disappears
like when a little girl says, "I don't believe in fairies,"
and at the bottom of the garden a family of fairies
grieve for their mum,
taken so young.

"We are all on life support machines," I tell the studio audience,
stomping on a Macbook.
"We are being drip fed by these tubes
having God-knows-what pumped into our veins."
Theatrically I unplug the USB cables I had carefully placed
in preparation for the analogy.

"Let's all quit Facebook!" I type as my status update
and we all count down together
"10, 9, 8 ..."
and after "3, 2, 1"
it's like when you've been in a traffic jam for so long
you say "Right!" and take off your seatbelt,
turn off the engine.

Ambition is like a bumbling tourist guide

You have no idea where he will take you.
"Follow me!" he says, waving an umbrella in the air,
and we all walk behind, in good faith.
"I'm pretty sure I know where I'm going," he says,

leading us from the city centre
through to a residential area where a lady pegs out her washing,
a man watering his plants eyes us with suspicion.
"Maybe this isn't the right way," our guide admits

"but I'm pretty sure if we take a shortcut through this field ..."
The man next to me tells me he was almost an airline pilot
as we wade through the muddy grass,
but he failed the final exam,

now he works at Autoglass in Nottingham.
"Dead end," our guide says, starting to get flustered
unfolding a map he takes from his rucksack.
A Japanese tourist puts the lens cap back on her camera.

We keep walking and our guide can't stop apologising,
"I'll go and ask the man in the shop," he says
and the rest of us sit in a park while we wait.
We talk about things we hope we'll live to see:

Prince Harry as King. The new Blur album.
A black Chancellor of the Exchequer.
A girl tells us she was runner up
in the UK Speedway Championship three years in a row

but she had to quit when she was diagnosed with epilepsy.
She shows everyone the medals she keeps in her coat pocket.
Our tourist guide comes back
and we explain that quite a few people have left,

saying they preferred to make their own way home.
"Never mind," he says, and we stay in the park a while,
admire the view from the top of the hill,
then carry on walking until we reach

an industrial estate. PC World. Carphone Warehouse.
Soon it's dark and there's only a few of us left. It's a bit awkward.
"Why are you still following me?"
the tourist guide asks, perplexed.

"It just feels too late to turn back now," I tell him.
"Let's keep going. I'm sure we'll get there in the end."

The continuity announcer stole my wife

We were on our second bottle of wine
when she went quiet, then said: "I've been cheating on you."
Just then the doorbell rang. It was our takeaway
but neither of us were hungry any more.

The man kept ringing the bell.
He must have known we were in
but this was no time for chow mein.
"Is it someone I know?" I asked
"Sort of," she said. "You know the bloke who says things like
And now, the snooker,
and Next on BBC 2: Eggheads. It's him."

She said it had been going on for two years
and I thought about all the times we'd been on the settee
waiting for Masterchef to start
and she didn't even flinch.
I hadn't suspected a thing.
I know she went away with work sometimes
but then so did I. I still feel guilty about the time
I drank everything in the mini-bar and called up a chatline,
but all the time she was shagging
the BBC2 continuity announcer.
I bet when he was saying "Next, Later with Jools Holland,"
he was thinking about her tits.

"Not the bloke on Dave?" my friend said when I told him.
"BBC 2," I said, and he nodded like it was Eton.
"Is he the bloke who says And now, Eggheads?" he asked.
He said "Do you think he has to wear a shirt and tie,
when he does his announcing,
or can he just wear something comfy like a jumper?
Do you think he just sits in a room with a TV and a microphone?
Do you think he can say what he wants,
or does he have to follow a script?"

There were so many questions I didn't have an answer to.
We didn't eat our takeaway
just threw the full plastic bag in the bin.
She went upstairs, packed her bags and left.
I always hoped she would come back
but she never did. And now whenever I watch BBC 2
I think how happy she must be
with the continuity announcer.
I still don't even know what he looks like.

The substitute goalkeeper

I go through life like a substitute goalkeeper.
If a girl I like starts seeing someone new
I think: well, let's see how this one copes,
with the swerving ball
and divots

when everyone knows it should be me out there
with a Number 1 on my back.
If I wait it out for long enough
he will make mistakes. Until then,
I will be as encouraging as I can,
I will look good in training.
My reputation can only be enhanced
by my non-appearances.

Then maybe people will start to notice my absence
my continued non-selection,
and feel sorry for me, dressed in full kit
on the bench during the game, waiting for a howler.
They will say: "Surely this guy deserves a chance by now?"

But if he plays a blinder, saves a penalty,
tips free kick after free kick over the bar
then I'll be the first to say "Well done,"

to admit that the best man won.
I'll go back to sitting on the bench
knowing there is no-one more forgettable
than the substitute goalkeeper of a winning team
and if I'm honest
sometimes I'm a bit scared of the ball.

The admin of being Prime Minister

There's a lot of admin to being Prime Minister.
The General Election doesn't just mean
a change of government,

it means moving into a new house
packing books into boxes
a new key on the key ring.

On your first day in Number 10
you need to read the instruction manual
for the central heating, work out how to get into the loft.

Can you still order things from Amazon?
Wouldn't someone at the depot look at the order
and do a double-take at the address?

How do you launch the missiles?
Is there a password?
Can you set it so it's the same

as your Yahoo account?
Where do you keep the Christmas decorations?
Is there tinsel that's been there since Thatcher?

What do you do if the Polish Foreign Minister wants to visit?
Does he have to stay at your house?
What will you talk about?

Do you have to go to war?
Think of the paperwork
all the extra meetings.

Have you got Sky?
Can you get Sky? All the channels?
You're the Prime Minister.

I know there will be staff to help you
but can you be confident running the country
if you don't know how your own radiators work?

No, no, no

After we broke up
I was up to my armpits in Sinead O'Connor
for weeks.
Every night I slept in my clothes
yet somehow still ended up wandering
round the supermarket in my pyjamas.

"I am in love with a girl called Jade," I told my tattooist,
but he knew that better than anyone.

"She'll come back," I said,
slapping myself across the face,
waking in the bath,
shivering in lukewarm water.

"I can't be depressed," I tell myself.
"I don't own a dressing gown."

"She does not want to go on holiday with you!"
the travel agent explained
taking the Eurostar brochures from me.
He asked me to stop coming in
it was breaking his heart.

"Just give me one more chance!" I started to write in a text,
but my phone was snatched from my hand.
"You've got to move on," I was told.
The London Community Gospel Choir were in my living room
wagging their fingers.
"It's over," they said,
and waited with me until I admitted they were right.
I had no idea I had so many chairs.

Firewall

He deals with problems
the same way he deals with the leaking tap in the bathroom;
just turns up his music until he can't hear
the drip, drip, drip.

He avoids confrontation like he avoids downloading viruses
uploads so many firewalls that nothing will get through
and he's got enough music on his computer
for this shuffle to last for generations.

He blocks out problems that aren't solved as easily
as downloading Orbital, Aphex Twin, Squarepusher,
thinking "I like that,"
and suddenly it's bouncing off his walls.

Problems are easy to avoid
if you go through life with your fingers in your ears
whenever there's a problem
you drop what you're holding
turn on your heels,
leg it in the opposite direction.

"I need to book that dentist's appointment," he thinks
every time he brushes his teeth,

but as soon as he swirls and spits he goes back to his room
closes the door, turns up his music
and the tap keeps dripping.

A boy called Michael Jackson

I used to play chess with a boy called Michael Jackson.
He wasn't very good at chess
but that was the least of his problems
and I've always felt sorry for him
unable to answer the most basic question:
"What's your name?"
"Michael Jackson."
Imagine the quips. Especially now.
"I thought you were dead!"
He can't even make a simple phone call
ringing up the BT Helpdesk
when they say "Can I take your name?"
he says "Michael Jackson,"
and there's a pause and he says
"Yes, like the singer.
No, you're not the first person to mention it.
Yes, it can be a bit annoying.
No, I don't know what my parents were thinking,
I guess they weren't familiar with the Jackson 5.
My dad works 50 hours a week as a neurosurgeon
and my mum is a full time carer for her brother
who has Down's Syndrome
I guess they're too busy to listen to disco."
When he first started to go to clubs
the bouncer would check his driving licence

call over to his mate: "This one's called Michael Jackson!"
And at the airport the man in the passport booth says
"Can you do the moonwalk?"
and Michael Jackson says "No,
I'm just going on holiday with my wife,"
and he'll say "What, Lisa Marie Presley?"
and he'll say "No, her name's Anne. Anne Jackson.
Try making a joke out of that."
There must be thousands of people
who all have to go through the same tedious conversations,
people called James Bond,
Harry Potter,
Julia Roberts,
Steve Davis,
Mark Thatcher,
Katie Price,
Fred West,
and little Michael Jackson
who says "No, I'm not the singer.
I'm just here for a game of chess."

Talking to machines

I don't like talking to these machines.
I always say the wrong thing and pause
and er and stutter too much.
Normally I don't bother to leave a message
but I thought I'd call to say how good it was
to see you the other morning
and I'm sorry I couldn't stick around for longer.
I just wanted to tell you
that I can't remember the last time I was in a good mood
the way I was for the rest of Thursday.
Two people at work commented on how I was chatty and smiling
and I thought, if this is the person I am
after just 45 minutes with you
drinking coffee while you're telling me about your job
then what would I be like if ...?
I don't like talking to these machines
and I know everyone says that, but for me it's just, well
I find it really hard. I hope you call back
but I know you once said you always delete your voicemails
without even listening to them
and maybe that's what's given me the confidence to leave this
knowing you'll probably never hear it,
or that maybe you'll listen, then press delete
and we can both pretend it never happened.

Frozen

"Why me?" I ask
waking five hundred years in the future
being told by a man in a white coat
that I have been cryogenically frozen

chosen as the one person to represent the twenty-first century.
"But you could have chosen a president or scientist
or film star," I say.
"I don't understand. I just work in an office."

"Oh," the man says, turning to his colleague.
"There may have been a mistake,"
and there is an awkward silence in the hovercar
on the way back to his cottage.

A go home moment

I was in the pub and waved at someone I knew
but didn't realise they were waving at someone else.
I was left there hanging
and I thought: the only thing I can do now is go home
and curl up in the foetal position
in the oven.

Hopefully he will have a few drinks and forget about it.
If I'm lucky something big will happen once I've gone,
a heart attack or something.
Maybe a stranger will go into labour
and he'll help deliver the baby,
the next day he'll be on the local news
the baby boy named after him.

Or perhaps on the way home he'll find a wallet,
hand it in at the police station at the end of the road
and they'll say "You can't stick around for a while can you?
We're one short for a line up."
and when the witness says, "That's the guy,
I'd recognise the bastard anywhere," he'll be taken to the cells
"You're going down for a long time," the cop will say.
"You'd better get used to drinking coffee from polystyrene cups."

Maybe hailstones will start smashing through the pub ceiling
more biblical than Moses.
"Follow me!" someone will say, running outside,
climbing down a manhole cover
and they'll all gather in a nuclear bunker
and see the Mayor in full regalia,
local celebrities playing computer games on beanbags.
"Were you followed?" the Mayoress would ask,
taking drinks orders.

The next time I see him I want to be able to say:
"It seems silly to mention it now,
after everything that happened when I left the pub,
but I didn't realise you were waving at someone else.
I thought you were waving at me."

Also by NASTY LITTLE PRESS